I0008270

Chapter 1: Understanding Dropshipping

What Is Dropshipping?

Dropshipping is a popular method of running an online business where the seller does not keep the products in stock. Instead, when a customer places an order, the seller purchases the product from a third party and has it shipped directly to the customer. This allows for a low overhead cost and eliminates the need for storage space, making it an attractive option for those looking to start their own online business.

Dropshipping 101: A Beginner's Guide to Starting Your Own Online Business

For beginners looking to get started in dropshipping, it is important to understand how the process works. Essentially, the seller creates an online store and lists products from suppliers. When a customer makes a purchase, the seller forwards the order to the supplier, who then ships the product directly to the customer. The seller makes a profit by marking up the price of the product, while the supplier handles the fulfillment and shipping.

Dropshipping 101: A Beginner's Guide to Starting Your Own Online Business

Advanced dropshipping strategies involve finding ways to optimize your business for maximum efficiency and profitability. This may include finding reliable suppliers, streamlining your order fulfillment process, and implementing marketing tactics to drive traffic to your online store. By continually learning and adapting to the ever-changing landscape of ecommerce, you can stay ahead of the competition and grow your dropshipping business.

Dropshipping 101: A Beginner's Guide to Starting Your Own Online Business

Dropshipping can be done on a variety of platforms, including Shopify and Amazon. Each platform has its own set of benefits and challenges, so it is important to research and choose the one that best fits your business model. By utilizing the tools and features provided by these platforms, you can streamline your dropshipping process and scale your business more effectively.

In conclusion, dropshipping offers a unique opportunity for individuals to start their own online business without the need for a large upfront investment. By understanding how dropshipping works, implementing advanced strategies, choosing the right platform, and continuously learning and adapting, you can build a successful dropshipping business that generates consistent profits and customer satisfaction.

How Does Dropshipping Work?

Dropshipping 101: A Beginner's Guide to Starting Your Own Online Business

Dropshipping is a popular business model that allows entrepreneurs to sell products online without having to hold inventory or handle shipping. But how exactly does dropshipping work? In simple terms, dropshipping involves a three-step process: the customer places an order on your online store, you forward the order to your supplier, and the supplier ships the product directly to the customer. This means that you never have to deal with the hassle of storing, packing, or shipping products yourself.

Dropshipping 101: A Beginner's Guide to Starting Your Own Online Business

For beginners looking to get started with dropshipping, it's important to understand the basics of how the process works. One key aspect is selecting a niche for your online store. This involves choosing a specific market or product category to focus on, which can help you target the right audience and stand out from competitors. Additionally, you'll need to source products from reliable suppliers who can fulfill orders quickly and efficiently. Researching potential suppliers and building relationships with them is crucial for ensuring smooth operations.

Dropshipping 101: A Beginner's Guide to Starting Your Own Online Business

As you become more experienced with dropshipping, you may want to explore advanced strategies to optimize your business. This could involve leveraging automation tools and software to streamline processes, implementing marketing tactics to drive traffic to your online store, or fine-tuning your pricing strategies to maximize profit margins. By continuously refining your approach and staying up-to-date with industry trends, you can increase your chances of success in the competitive dropshipping market.

Dropshipping 101: A Beginner's Guide to Starting Your Own Online Business

When it comes to specific platforms for dropshipping, popular options include Shopify and Amazon. These platforms offer user-friendly interfaces, built-in tools for managing orders and inventory, and a wide range of integrations with suppliers and marketing channels. By choosing the platform that best fits your needs and goals, you can create a professional and efficient online store that attracts customers and drives sales.

In conclusion, dropshipping offers a flexible and low-risk way to start an online business. By understanding how dropshipping works, selecting the right niche, sourcing quality products, and implementing effective strategies, you can build a successful dropshipping venture. Whether you're a beginner looking to get started or an experienced entrepreneur seeking to grow your business, there are endless opportunities to thrive in the dynamic world of dropshipping.

Benefits of Dropshipping

Dropshipping 101: A Beginner's Guide to Starting Your Own Online Business

Dropshipping is a popular business model that offers numerous benefits to entrepreneurs looking to start their own online business. One of the main advantages of dropshipping is that it requires minimal upfront investment. Unlike traditional retail businesses, dropshipping does not require you to purchase inventory in bulk or invest in storage space. This means that you can start your online store with little to no capital, making it an ideal option for those looking to test the waters of entrepreneurship without taking on significant financial risk.

Dropshipping 101: A Beginner's Guide to Starting Your Own Online Business

Another key benefit of dropshipping is the flexibility it offers in terms of product selection. With dropshipping, you can easily test different products and niches to see what resonates with your target audience. This flexibility allows you to quickly pivot and adapt to changing market trends, ensuring that your online store remains competitive and profitable in the long run. Additionally, dropshipping allows you to work with multiple suppliers, giving you access to a wide range of products without having to manage inventory or shipping logistics yourself.

Dropshipping also offers scalability, allowing you to grow your online business at your own pace. As your store grows and attracts more customers, you can easily expand your product offerings and reach new markets without the need for additional investment in inventory or infrastructure. This scalability makes dropshipping an attractive option for entrepreneurs looking to build a sustainable and profitable online business over time.

In addition to these benefits, dropshipping also provides opportunities for automation and efficiency. By using dropshipping automation tools and software, you can streamline your order fulfillment process, track inventory levels, and manage customer inquiries with ease. This automation not only saves you time and resources but also allows you to focus on growing your business and increasing your profits. With the right tools and strategies in place, dropshipping can be a highly profitable and rewarding venture for entrepreneurs of all levels of experience.

Overall, dropshipping offers a host of benefits for entrepreneurs looking to start their own online business. From minimal upfront investment and flexibility in product selection to scalability and automation opportunities, dropshipping provides a low-risk and high-reward path to building a successful online store. By understanding the benefits of dropshipping and implementing effective strategies, entrepreneurs can create a thriving online business that generates sustainable income and long-term success.

Drawbacks of Dropshipping

Dropshipping 101: A Beginner's Guide to Starting Your Own Online Business

While dropshipping can be a lucrative business model for many entrepreneurs, there are also some drawbacks to consider before diving in. One of the main drawbacks of dropshipping is the lack of control over inventory. Since you are relying on suppliers to fulfill orders, you may run into issues with stock availability or shipping delays, which can lead to unhappy customers.

Another drawback of dropshipping is the lower profit margins compared to traditional retail models. Since you are not purchasing products in bulk upfront, you may not be able to negotiate lower wholesale prices, resulting in thinner profit margins. This can make it challenging to scale your business and reinvest in growth.

Dropshipping 101: A Beginner's Guide to Starting Your Own Online Business

Additionally, with dropshipping, you may also face increased competition and saturation in certain niches. As dropshipping continues to gain popularity, more and more entrepreneurs are entering the market, making it harder to stand out and attract customers. It's essential to carefully research and select a niche with less competition and high demand to increase your chances of success.

Another potential drawback of dropshipping is the reliance on third-party suppliers for product quality and customer service. If a supplier fails to deliver on time or provides low-quality products, it can reflect poorly on your brand and lead to negative reviews and customer dissatisfaction. It's crucial to thoroughly vet and establish strong relationships with reliable suppliers to mitigate this risk.

Lastly, dropshipping can also require a significant amount of time and effort to manage effectively. From sourcing products and managing inventory to handling customer inquiries and marketing, running a successful dropshipping business can be demanding. It's essential to have a solid plan in place and use automation tools and software to streamline processes and free up your time for other aspects of your business.

Chapter 2: Dropshipping for Beginners

Setting Up Your Online Store

Dropshipping 101: A Beginner's Guide to Starting Your Own Online Business

Setting up your online store is a crucial step in launching your dropshipping business. Before you can start selling products, you need to create a professional and user-friendly website that will attract customers and drive sales. The first thing you'll need to do is choose a platform to host your online store. Popular options include Shopify, WooCommerce, and BigCommerce. Each platform has its own set of features and pricing, so be sure to choose one that fits your needs and budget.

Dropshipping 101: A Beginner's Guide to Starting Your Own Online Business

Once you've selected a platform, you'll need to design your online store. This includes choosing a theme, adding products, writing product descriptions, and setting up payment gateways. Your online store should be visually appealing, easy to navigate, and optimized for mobile devices. Remember, first impressions are crucial in the world of e-commerce, so take the time to create a professional-looking website that instills trust in your customers.

Dropshipping 101: A Beginner's Guide to Starting Your Own Online Business

After setting up your online store, you'll need to focus on product sourcing. This involves finding reliable suppliers who can provide high-quality products at competitive prices. One popular option is to use dropshipping suppliers, who will fulfill orders on your behalf and ship directly to your customers. Be sure to research potential suppliers and choose ones that offer fast shipping, good customer service, and a wide selection of products.

Dropshipping 101: A Beginner's Guide to Starting Your Own Online Business

Marketing your online store is essential for driving traffic and generating sales. There are many different marketing tactics you can use, including social media advertising, influencer marketing, email marketing, and search engine optimization. Experiment with different strategies to see what works best for your business. Remember, consistency is key when it comes to marketing, so be sure to regularly promote your products and engage with your audience.

In conclusion, setting up your online store is an important step in starting a successful dropshipping business. By choosing the right platform, designing a professional website, sourcing high-quality products, and implementing effective marketing tactics, you can attract customers, drive sales, and grow your business. Remember, success in dropshipping takes time and effort, so be patient and persistent as you work towards building a profitable online store.

Finding Reliable Suppliers

Dropshipping 101: A Beginner's Guide to Starting Your Own Online Business

When starting a dropshipping business, one of the most important steps is finding reliable suppliers. Your suppliers play a crucial role in the success of your business, as they are responsible for fulfilling orders and ensuring timely delivery to your customers. In this subchapter, we will discuss how to find trustworthy suppliers that will help you build a successful dropshipping business.

Dropshipping 101: A Beginner's Guide to Starting Your Own Online Business

The first step in finding reliable suppliers is to conduct thorough research. Look for suppliers that have a good reputation in the industry and are known for their quality products and reliable shipping. You can start by searching online directories, such as SaleHoo or Worldwide Brands, which list reputable suppliers in various niches. You can also reach out to other dropshippers in your network for recommendations on reliable suppliers they have worked with in the past.

Once you have identified potential suppliers, it is important to vet them thoroughly. Check their customer reviews and ratings to ensure they have a track record of delivering high-quality products and excellent customer service. You should also request samples of their products to assess their quality firsthand. Additionally, inquire about their shipping times and policies to ensure they can meet your customers' expectations.

Another important consideration when choosing suppliers is their pricing and payment terms. Make sure to compare prices from different suppliers to ensure you are getting the best deal for your products. Additionally, clarify their payment terms, including any upfront costs or fees, to avoid any surprises down the line. It is also important to establish clear communication channels with your suppliers to address any issues or concerns that may arise during the fulfillment process.

In conclusion, finding reliable suppliers is crucial for the success of your dropshipping business. By conducting thorough research, vetting potential suppliers, and negotiating favorable terms, you can build a strong relationship with your suppliers that will help you grow your business. Remember that reliability, quality, and good communication are key factors to consider when selecting suppliers for your dropshipping business.

Choosing Profitable Products

Dropshipping 101: A Beginner's Guide to Starting Your Own Online Business

When it comes to starting a successful dropshipping business, one of the most crucial steps is choosing profitable products to sell. This process involves thorough research and analysis to identify products that have high demand and low competition in the market. By selecting the right products, you can increase your chances of achieving success and profitability in your online business.

Dropshipping 101: A Beginner's Guide to Starting Your Own Online Business

To begin the process of choosing profitable products for your dropshipping business, it is important to first understand your target audience and niche market. Consider the interests, needs, and preferences of your potential customers to determine what types of products are likely to appeal to them. By focusing on a specific niche, you can tailor your product selection to meet the demands of a particular group of consumers, making it easier to attract and retain customers.

Dropshipping 101: A Beginner's Guide to Starting Your Own Online Business

Once you have identified your target audience and niche market, research trending products and popular categories within that market. Look for products that have a high search volume, low competition, and a consistent demand over time. By staying up-to-date on current trends and consumer preferences, you can identify profitable products that are likely to attract customers and generate sales for your dropshipping business.

In addition to researching trends and market demand, it is also important to consider the profit margins and pricing strategies for the products you are considering selling. Look for products with a healthy profit margin that will allow you to make a reasonable profit while remaining competitive in the market. Consider factors such as shipping costs, supplier prices, and market prices when setting your pricing strategy to ensure that you are able to maximize your profits while offering competitive prices to customers.

Ultimately, the key to choosing profitable products for your dropshipping business is to combine thorough research, market analysis, and strategic planning. By understanding your target audience, niche market, and product trends, you can identify products that are likely to be successful and profitable in your online business. By selecting the right products and implementing effective pricing strategies, you can increase your chances of achieving success and profitability as a dropshipper.

Managing Orders and Inventory

Dropshipping 101: A Beginner's Guide to Starting Your Own Online Business

Managing Orders and Inventory is a crucial aspect of running a successful dropshipping business. In this subchapter, we will explore the key strategies and best practices for effectively managing your orders and inventory to ensure smooth operations and maximize profitability.

Dropshipping 101: A Beginner's Guide to Starting Your Own Online Business

One of the first steps in managing orders and inventory is to establish a reliable system for tracking and processing incoming orders. This includes setting up an efficient order management system that allows you to easily track and fulfill customer orders in a timely manner. It is important to stay organized and keep track of inventory levels to avoid overselling and stockouts.

In addition to tracking orders, it is essential to carefully monitor and manage your inventory levels to ensure that you have enough stock on hand to fulfill customer orders. Implementing a robust inventory management system can help you keep track of your stock levels, identify slow-moving products, and make informed decisions about restocking and product selection.

Dropshipping 101: A Beginner's Guide to Starting Your Own Online Business

To streamline the order fulfillment process, consider using automation tools and software that can help you manage orders, track inventory, and streamline the shipping process. By leveraging technology and automation, you can save time and resources while improving the overall efficiency of your dropshipping operations.

By effectively managing your orders and inventory, you can ensure that your customers receive their orders in a timely manner, minimize the risk of stockouts and overselling, and maintain a positive reputation for your dropshipping business. Implementing best practices for managing orders and inventory is key to achieving long-term success in the competitive world of dropshipping.

Chapter 3: Advanced Dropshipping Strategies

Building a Brand Identity

Dropshipping 101: A Beginner's Guide to Starting Your Own Online Business

Building a strong brand identity is essential for any dropshipping business looking to stand out in a competitive market. Your brand identity is what sets you apart from the competition and helps to establish trust and credibility with your customers. It is important to carefully consider every aspect of your brand, from your logo and color scheme to your messaging and customer service.

Dropshipping 101: A Beginner's Guide to Starting Your Own Online Business

One key aspect of building a brand identity is consistency. Your brand should be consistent across all platforms, from your website to your social media profiles. This includes using the same logo, color scheme, and messaging to create a cohesive and recognizable brand image. Consistency helps to build trust with your customers and makes your brand more memorable.

Another important aspect of building a brand identity is defining your target audience. Understanding who your ideal customer is can help you tailor your branding and marketing efforts to appeal to their specific needs and preferences. By knowing your target audience, you can create a brand identity that resonates with them and makes them more likely to engage with your business.

In addition to consistency and defining your target audience, it is also important to differentiate your brand from the competition. This can be done by highlighting what sets your business apart, whether it's your unique product offerings, exceptional customer service, or innovative marketing tactics. By clearly communicating your unique value proposition, you can attract customers who are looking for what makes your brand special.

Ultimately, building a strong brand identity is an ongoing process that requires dedication and attention to detail. By focusing on consistency, defining your target audience, and differentiating your brand from the competition, you can create a brand identity that resonates with your customers and helps your dropshipping business succeed.

Implementing SEO Techniques

Dropshipping 101: A Beginner's Guide to Starting Your Own Online Business

Implementing SEO techniques is crucial for the success of your dropshipping business. SEO, or search engine optimization, is the process of optimizing your website to rank higher in search engine results pages. By implementing SEO techniques, you can increase your website's visibility and attract more organic traffic.

Dropshipping 101: A Beginner's Guide to Starting Your Own Online Business

One of the most important SEO techniques is keyword research. Keyword research involves identifying the keywords and phrases that your target audience is searching for online. By incorporating these keywords into your website content, meta tags, and URLs, you can improve your website's visibility in search engine results pages.

Dropshipping 101: A Beginner's Guide to Starting Your Own Online Business

Another important SEO technique is optimizing your website's on-page elements. This includes optimizing your website's title tags, meta descriptions, and headings to make them more search engine-friendly. By optimizing these elements, you can improve your website's chances of ranking higher in search engine results pages.

Off-page SEO techniques are also important for improving your website's search engine rankings. This includes building backlinks from reputable websites, creating social media profiles, and engaging with online communities. By implementing these off-page SEO techniques, you can improve your website's authority and credibility in the eyes of search engines.

Overall, implementing SEO techniques is essential for the success of your dropshipping business. By optimizing your website for search engines, you can attract more organic traffic, increase your website's visibility, and ultimately drive more sales. So, take the time to implement SEO techniques into your dropshipping business strategy and watch your online business thrive.

Utilizing Social Media Marketing

Dropshipping 101: A Beginner's Guide to Starting Your Own Online Business

Utilizing Social Media Marketing is a crucial aspect of running a successful dropshipping business in today's digital age. Social media platforms such as Facebook, Instagram, Twitter, and Pinterest offer a wealth of opportunities to connect with potential customers and drive traffic to your online store. By leveraging the power of social media marketing, you can greatly increase your brand's visibility and reach a wider audience.

One of the key benefits of utilizing social media marketing for your dropshipping business is the ability to target specific demographics and interests. With advanced targeting options available on platforms like Facebook and Instagram, you can create highly targeted ads that reach the right audience for your products. This can help increase the likelihood of converting viewers into customers, ultimately driving sales and boosting your bottom line.

Dropshipping 101: A Beginner's Guide to Starting Your Own Online Business

In addition to targeted advertising, social media marketing also allows you to engage with your audience on a more personal level. By posting regular updates, sharing behind-the-scenes content, and responding to comments and messages, you can build a loyal following of customers who trust and value your brand. This can lead to repeat purchases and word-of-mouth referrals, further growing your business over time.

Dropshipping 101: A Beginner's Guide to Starting Your Own Online Business

When it comes to social media marketing for dropshipping, it's important to have a well-thought-out strategy in place. This includes setting clear goals, identifying your target audience, creating compelling content, and tracking your results to measure success. By consistently posting engaging content, running promotions and giveaways, and collaborating with influencers in your niche, you can effectively grow your following and drive sales through social media channels.

Overall, social media marketing is a powerful tool that can help you take your dropshipping business to the next level. By utilizing the various platforms and strategies available, you can increase brand awareness, drive traffic to your online store, and ultimately boost sales and revenue. With the right approach and a commitment to consistency, social media marketing can be a game-changer for your dropshipping business.

Scaling Your Dropshipping Business

Dropshipping 101: A Beginner's Guide to Starting Your Own Online Business

Once you have successfully set up your dropshipping business, the next step is to focus on scaling your operations to increase your revenue and reach a wider audience. Scaling your dropshipping business involves expanding your product offerings, optimizing your marketing strategies, and streamlining your operations to handle a higher volume of sales.

One of the key strategies for scaling your dropshipping business is to diversify your product range. By offering a wider variety of products, you can attract a larger customer base and increase your chances of making sales. Research popular trends and niche markets to identify new products to add to your store and keep your offerings fresh and appealing to customers.

Dropshipping 101: A Beginner's Guide to Starting Your Own Online Business

Another important aspect of scaling your dropshipping business is to optimize your marketing tactics. Invest in targeted advertising campaigns on social media platforms, search engines, and other relevant channels to reach potential customers and drive traffic to your online store. Utilize analytics tools to track the performance of your marketing efforts and make adjustments as needed to improve your conversion rates.

Dropshipping 101: A Beginner's Guide to Starting Your Own Online Business

In order to handle the increased volume of sales that comes with scaling your dropshipping business, it is essential to streamline your operations. Consider investing in automation tools and software to automate repetitive tasks such as order processing, inventory management, and customer service. This will help you save time and resources while improving the efficiency of your business operations.

Dropshipping 101: A Beginner's Guide to Starting Your Own Online Business

As you scale your dropshipping business, it is important to focus on maintaining high levels of customer service and satisfaction. Respond promptly to customer inquiries and concerns, provide accurate and up-to-date information about products, and ensure timely delivery of orders. Building a positive reputation for excellent customer service will help you retain existing customers and attract new ones through word-of-mouth referrals.

By implementing these strategies for scaling your dropshipping business, you can take your online store to the next level and achieve sustainable growth and success in the competitive e-commerce landscape. Stay informed about the latest trends and best practices in dropshipping, and continue to adapt and evolve your business to meet the changing needs and expectations of your customers.

Chapter 4: Dropshipping on Specific Platforms

Dropshipping on Shopify

Dropshipping 101: A Beginner's Guide to Starting Your Own Online Business

Dropshipping on Shopify is a popular choice among entrepreneurs looking to start their own online business. Shopify is a user-friendly platform that allows you to easily set up your online store and sell products without the need to hold inventory. In this subchapter, we will explore the ins and outs of dropshipping on Shopify and how you can make it work for you.

Dropshipping 101: A Beginner's Guide to Starting Your Own Online Business

When it comes to dropshipping for beginners, Shopify is a great option because it offers a range of tools and features to help you get started. You can choose from a variety of themes and templates to design your store, and Shopify's built-in payment processing makes it easy for customers to make purchases. Additionally, Shopify integrates with various dropshipping apps and suppliers, making it simple to find products to sell and fulfill orders.

Dropshipping 101: A Beginner's Guide to Starting Your Own Online Business

For those looking to take their
dropshipping business to the next level,
advanced strategies on Shopify can help
you stand out from the competition. You
can use Shopify's marketing tools to drive
traffic to your store, optimize your
product listings for search engines, and
implement email marketing campaigns
to keep customers engaged. With the
right tactics, you can increase sales and
build a loyal customer base.

Dropshipping 101: A Beginner's Guide to Starting Your Own Online Business

When it comes to dropshipping on specific platforms like Shopify, it's important to carefully select your niche and products. Research trending products and analyze market demand to find a profitable niche to focus on. Consider factors like profit margins, competition, and target audience when choosing products to sell on Shopify.

In conclusion, dropshipping on Shopify offers a wealth of opportunities for entrepreneurs looking to start their own online business. By utilizing Shopify's features and tools, you can create a successful dropshipping store that generates consistent sales and revenue. Whether you're a beginner or looking to expand your dropshipping business, Shopify provides the resources you need to succeed in the competitive e-commerce landscape.

Dropshipping on Amazon

Dropshipping 101: A Beginner's Guide to Starting Your Own Online Business

Dropshipping on Amazon is a popular method used by many online entrepreneurs to start their own e-commerce business without the need for inventory storage or upfront costs. In this subchapter, we will explore how dropshipping on Amazon works and the strategies you can implement to be successful in this competitive marketplace.

Dropshipping 101: A Beginner's Guide to Starting Your Own Online Business

One of the key advantages of dropshipping on Amazon is the large customer base it offers. With millions of active users on the platform, you have the opportunity to reach a wide audience and potentially increase your sales. However, with this vast reach comes intense competition, so it is crucial to differentiate yourself and stand out from other sellers.

Dropshipping 101: A Beginner's Guide to Starting Your Own Online Business

To begin dropshipping on Amazon, you will need to set up an account and list your products on the platform. It is important to choose products that are in demand and have a high profit margin to maximize your earnings. Additionally, optimizing your product listings with relevant keywords and high-quality images can help improve your visibility and attract more customers.

Dropshipping 101: A Beginner's Guide to Starting Your Own Online Business

Advanced dropshipping strategies on Amazon involve leveraging data analytics, optimizing your pricing strategy, and implementing automation tools to streamline your operations. By analyzing market trends and consumer behavior, you can make informed decisions to improve your sales performance and stay ahead of the competition.

In conclusion, dropshipping on Amazon can be a lucrative business opportunity for those willing to put in the time and effort to succeed. By understanding the platform's unique features and implementing effective strategies, you can build a profitable online business and achieve your entrepreneurial goals.

Dropshipping on eBay

Dropshipping on eBay can be a lucrative business venture for individuals looking to start their own online business. eBay is a popular e-commerce platform that allows sellers to list products for sale without having to hold inventory. This means that sellers can work with suppliers to fulfill orders directly to customers, eliminating the need for warehousing and shipping products themselves.

Dropshipping 101: A Beginner's Guide to Starting Your Own Online Business

For beginners, dropshipping on eBay can be a great way to dip your toes into the world of e-commerce. By setting up an eBay seller account and finding reliable suppliers, you can start listing products and making sales in no time. It's important to research popular products and niches on eBay to find out what sells well and what customers are looking for.

Advanced dropshipping strategies on eBay involve optimizing your listings for search engines, utilizing eBay's promoted listings feature, and offering exceptional customer service. By constantly monitoring your sales and adjusting your strategies accordingly, you can maximize your profits and grow your business on eBay.

When dropshipping on eBay, it's important to stay up-to-date on the platform's policies and guidelines to avoid any potential issues. Additionally, building a strong reputation as a seller through excellent customer service and fast shipping times can help boost your sales and attract repeat customers.

Overall, dropshipping on eBay can be a profitable and rewarding business opportunity for entrepreneurs in the e-commerce space. By learning the ins and outs of the platform, staying informed on industry trends, and continuously improving your strategies, you can achieve success and build a thriving online business on eBay.

Dropshipping on Etsy

Dropshipping 101: A Beginner's Guide to Starting Your Own Online Business

Dropshipping on Etsy is a popular choice for many online entrepreneurs looking to start their own e-commerce business. Etsy is a marketplace known for unique, handmade, and vintage items, making it a great platform for dropshipping niche products. In this subchapter, we will explore how dropshipping on Etsy works and the strategies you can use to succeed in this competitive marketplace.

To begin dropshipping on Etsy, you first need to set up an Etsy shop and list your products for sale. Unlike other platforms, Etsy has specific guidelines for dropshipping, so it's important to familiarize yourself with their policies before getting started. Once your shop is set up, you can start sourcing products from suppliers to list in your Etsy store. Many dropshippers on Etsy choose to sell niche products that cater to a specific audience, such as handmade jewelry, personalized gifts, or eco-friendly home goods.

Dropshipping 101: A Beginner's Guide to Starting Your Own Online Business

For beginners, it's essential to do thorough research on your target market and competition before diving into dropshipping on Etsy. Understanding what customers are looking for and how your products can stand out from the competition will help you create a successful Etsy shop. Additionally, utilizing SEO strategies to optimize your product listings and leveraging social media marketing can help drive traffic to your Etsy store and increase sales.

Dropshipping 101: A Beginner's Guide to Starting Your Own Online Business

Advanced dropshipping strategies on Etsy may include expanding your product range, collaborating with influencers or bloggers for promotion, and utilizing Etsy's advertising platform to reach a larger audience. By continuously testing and optimizing your strategies, you can stay ahead of the competition and grow your dropshipping business on Etsy.

Dropshipping 101: A Beginner's Guide to Starting Your Own Online Business

In conclusion, dropshipping on Etsy offers a unique opportunity for online entrepreneurs to tap into a niche market and build a successful e-commerce business. By understanding how dropshipping works on Etsy, implementing effective marketing strategies, and providing excellent customer service, you can create a profitable and sustainable online business. With dedication and perseverance, you can achieve success as a dropshipper on Etsy and join the ranks of other entrepreneurs who have found success on this platform.

Chapter 5: Dropshipping Niche Selection

Researching Profitable Niches

Researching profitable niches is a crucial step in building a successful dropshipping business. Before diving into the world of online retail, it is essential to understand what a niche is and why it is important. A niche is a specific segment of the market that caters to a particular group of customers with unique needs and preferences. By focusing on a niche market, you can target a specific audience and set yourself apart from the competition.

Dropshipping 101: A Beginner's Guide to Starting Your Own Online Business

When researching profitable niches for your dropshipping business, it is important to consider factors such as market demand, competition, and profitability. Look for niches that have a high demand but low competition, as this will increase your chances of success. Additionally, consider the profit margins and pricing strategies of different niches to ensure that you can make a profit while offering competitive prices to your customers.

Dropshipping 101: A Beginner's Guide to Starting Your Own Online Business

One effective strategy for researching profitable niches is to use online tools and resources to analyze market trends and consumer behavior. Platforms such as Google Trends, Amazon Best Sellers, and social media platforms can provide valuable insights into popular products and niches. By leveraging these tools, you can identify emerging trends and capitalize on profitable opportunities before they become saturated.

In addition to using online tools, it is also helpful to conduct market research and gather feedback from potential customers. Consider conducting surveys, focus groups, or interviews to understand the needs and preferences of your target audience. By listening to your customers and adapting your product offerings to meet their needs, you can build a loyal customer base and drive sales.

Overall, researching profitable niches is a critical step in building a successful dropshipping business. By focusing on niche markets with high demand, low competition, and strong profit potential, you can set yourself up for long-term success in the world of online retail. Remember to leverage online tools, conduct market research, and listen to your customers to identify profitable niches and drive sales in your dropshipping business.

Analyzing Competition

Analyzing competition is a crucial aspect of running a successful dropshipping business. Understanding who your competitors are, what they offer, and how they operate can provide valuable insights that can help you differentiate your business and attract customers. By analyzing your competition, you can identify gaps in the market, discover new product opportunities, and develop strategies to stay ahead in the competitive landscape.

Dropshipping 101: A Beginner's Guide to Starting Your Own Online Business

One key aspect of analyzing competition in dropshipping is conducting a thorough market research. This involves identifying your direct competitors – other dropshipping businesses selling similar products in the same niche – as well as indirect competitors such as traditional retailers and online marketplaces. By studying their pricing strategies, product offerings, marketing tactics, and customer service practices, you can gain a better understanding of the competitive landscape and identify areas where you can improve and differentiate your business.

Another important aspect of analyzing competition is monitoring and tracking your competitors' performance. This involves keeping an eye on their sales, customer reviews, social media presence, and overall brand reputation. By staying informed about what your competitors are doing, you can identify trends, spot opportunities, and make data-driven decisions to optimize your own business and stay competitive in the market.

In addition to studying your competitors, it's also important to analyze your own strengths and weaknesses. By conducting a SWOT analysis (Strengths, Weaknesses, Opportunities, Threats), you can identify areas where you excel and areas where you need to improve. This self-assessment can help you develop a clear strategy for positioning your business in the market, leveraging your strengths, and addressing any weaknesses that may be hindering your success.

Overall, analyzing competition is a continuous process that requires ongoing monitoring, research, and strategic planning. By understanding your competitors, staying informed about market trends, and leveraging your own strengths, you can position your dropshipping business for success and stay ahead in the competitive landscape. Remember, competition is not something to be feared, but rather an opportunity to learn, grow, and thrive in the world of dropshipping.

Identifying Trends

Identifying trends is a crucial aspect of running a successful dropshipping business. By staying ahead of the curve and understanding what products are in demand, you can maximize your profits and attract more customers. There are several ways to identify trends in the dropshipping industry, including monitoring social media platforms, keeping an eye on popular search engines, and utilizing tools like Google Trends.

Dropshipping 101: A Beginner's Guide to Starting Your Own Online Business

One effective way to identify trends in dropshipping is by paying attention to what is popular on social media platforms such as Instagram, Facebook, and TikTok. By monitoring what influencers and consumers are talking about and sharing, you can get a sense of what products are currently trending. Additionally, social media platforms often have features that allow you to see which products are getting the most engagement, which can be a valuable source of information for identifying trends.

Another useful tool for identifying trends in dropshipping is Google Trends, which allows you to see how popular a certain search term is over time. By entering relevant keywords related to your niche, you can see if interest in certain products is on the rise or decline. This can help you make informed decisions about which products to sell and which trends to capitalize on.

Dropshipping 101: A Beginner's Guide to Starting Your Own Online Business

In addition to social media and Google Trends, keeping an eye on popular search engines like Amazon can also help you identify trends in the dropshipping industry. By looking at the top-selling products in your niche, you can get a sense of what customers are currently interested in and adjust your product offerings accordingly. This can help you stay competitive in the ever-changing world of dropshipping.

Overall, identifying trends is a key component of running a successful dropshipping business. By utilizing tools like social media platforms, Google Trends, and popular search engines, you can stay ahead of the curve and make informed decisions about which products to sell. By keeping a close eye on trends in the industry, you can maximize your profits and attract more customers to your online store.

Testing and Validating Your Niche

Dropshipping 101: A Beginner's Guide to Starting Your Own Online Business

Testing and validating your niche is a crucial step in the dropshipping business journey. Before diving in headfirst, it's important to ensure that your chosen niche is viable and will attract customers. This process involves conducting thorough market research and testing different products within your niche to see what resonates with your target audience.

Dropshipping 101: A Beginner's Guide to Starting Your Own Online Business

One way to test your niche is by creating a small test store or landing page to gauge interest. This allows you to see how many people are interested in your products and if there is potential for profit. You can also use tools like Google Trends and keyword research to see if there is a demand for your niche and products.

In addition to testing your niche, it's important to validate it by analyzing the competition. Take a look at other dropshipping stores in your niche and see what they are doing well and where they may be falling short. This will help you identify gaps in the market and areas where you can differentiate yourself.

Another important aspect of testing and validating your niche is understanding your target audience. Conduct surveys, polls, and interviews to gather feedback and insights from potential customers. This will help you tailor your products and marketing strategies to better meet the needs and preferences of your target market.

Overall, testing and validating your niche is a critical step in ensuring the success of your dropshipping business. By taking the time to thoroughly research and analyze your niche, you can set yourself up for long-term success and profitability in the competitive world of ecommerce.

Chapter 6: Dropshipping Product Sourcing

Finding Reliable Suppliers

Dropshipping 101: A Beginner's Guide to Starting Your Own Online Business

When starting a dropshipping business, one of the most crucial steps is finding reliable suppliers to work with. Your suppliers will be responsible for fulfilling orders and delivering products to your customers, so it's important to choose them wisely. To find reliable suppliers, start by researching different suppliers in your niche. Look for suppliers with good reviews and a track record of on-time delivery. You can also reach out to other dropshippers in your industry for recommendations on suppliers they trust.

Dropshipping 101: A Beginner's Guide to Starting Your Own Online Business

Once you have a list of potential suppliers, take the time to vet them thoroughly. Check their reputation online, read customer reviews, and ask for references if possible. It's also a good idea to order samples from each supplier to test the quality of their products and their shipping times. By doing your due diligence upfront, you can avoid potential headaches down the line with unreliable suppliers.

When choosing a supplier, consider factors such as their pricing, shipping times, and customer service. You'll want to work with suppliers who offer competitive pricing so that you can maximize your profit margins. It's also important to choose suppliers who can ship products quickly and provide excellent customer service in case any issues arise with orders. By prioritizing these factors, you can ensure a smooth and successful partnership with your suppliers.

Dropshipping 101: A Beginner's Guide to Starting Your Own Online Business

In addition to researching and vetting suppliers, it's also a good idea to diversify your supplier base. Working with multiple suppliers can help you mitigate risks such as stockouts or shipping delays. By spreading your orders across different suppliers, you can ensure that you always have access to the products you need to fulfill customer orders. This approach also allows you to test different suppliers and find the ones that best meet your needs in terms of pricing, quality, and reliability.

Overall, finding reliable suppliers is a key component of building a successful dropshipping business. By taking the time to research, vet, and diversify your supplier base, you can set your business up for long-term success. Remember that building strong relationships with your suppliers is also important, as it can lead to better pricing, faster shipping times, and overall better service for your customers. With the right suppliers in place, you can focus on growing your business and providing a great experience for your customers.

Negotiating Wholesale Prices

Dropshipping 101: A Beginner's Guide to Starting Your Own Online Business

Negotiating wholesale prices is a crucial aspect of running a successful dropshipping business. When you are able to secure lower prices from your suppliers, you can increase your profit margins and remain competitive in the market. In this subchapter, we will discuss some tips and strategies for negotiating wholesale prices effectively.

Dropshipping 101: A Beginner's Guide to Starting Your Own Online Business

One of the first steps in negotiating wholesale prices is to research and compare prices from different suppliers. By having a good understanding of the market prices for the products you are selling, you can better negotiate with your suppliers. You can also leverage this information to negotiate better deals and ensure that you are getting the best possible prices for your products.

Dropshipping 101: A Beginner's Guide to Starting Your Own Online Business

Another tip for negotiating wholesale prices is to build a strong relationship with your suppliers. By establishing a good rapport with your suppliers, you can create a more collaborative and mutually beneficial relationship. This can lead to better pricing, faster shipping times, and access to exclusive deals and products.

It is also important to be prepared and have a clear understanding of your costs and profit margins before entering into negotiations with your suppliers. By knowing your numbers and being able to demonstrate how a lower wholesale price will benefit both parties, you can increase your chances of securing a better deal.

Dropshipping 101: A Beginner's Guide to Starting Your Own Online Business

Lastly, don't be afraid to negotiate and ask for discounts or better terms. Suppliers are often willing to negotiate, especially if they see the potential for a long-term partnership with your business. Remember to be confident, professional, and respectful during negotiations to build a positive relationship with your suppliers.

In conclusion, negotiating wholesale prices is an essential skill for any dropshipping business owner. By researching, building relationships, being prepared, and confidently negotiating with suppliers, you can secure better prices, increase your profit margins, and ultimately, grow your business successfully.

Ensuring Product Quality

Ensuring product quality is a crucial aspect of running a successful dropshipping business. When customers receive their orders, they expect the products to meet their expectations in terms of quality and functionality. Failing to deliver on this can result in negative reviews, customer complaints, and ultimately, loss of business. Therefore, it is essential for every person involved in dropshipping to prioritize product quality at all times.

Dropshipping 101: A Beginner's Guide to Starting Your Own Online Business

One way to ensure product quality is to carefully vet and select reliable suppliers. Before partnering with a supplier, it is important to conduct thorough research, read reviews, and even order sample products to assess the quality firsthand. By working with reputable suppliers who prioritize quality control, you can minimize the risk of receiving subpar products and ensure that your customers are satisfied with their purchases.

Another key aspect of ensuring product quality is to regularly inspect and test the products you are selling. This can involve conducting quality control checks before shipping out orders, inspecting products upon arrival at your warehouse (if applicable), and seeking feedback from customers to identify any potential issues. By staying proactive and addressing quality concerns promptly, you can uphold a positive reputation for your business and build trust with your customers.

Dropshipping 101: A Beginner's Guide to Starting Your Own Online Business

In addition to vetting suppliers and inspecting products, it is also important to provide accurate product descriptions and images on your online store. Clearly communicate product specifications, features, and any potential limitations to set realistic expectations for customers. By being transparent about what customers can expect from their purchases, you can reduce the likelihood of returns or disputes related to product quality.

Ultimately, ensuring product quality is not just about meeting customer expectations – it is also about building a strong brand reputation and fostering customer loyalty. By consistently delivering high-quality products and exceptional customer service, you can differentiate your business from competitors, attract repeat customers, and ultimately drive long-term success in the world of dropshipping.

Handling Returns and Refunds

Dropshipping 101: A Beginner's Guide to Starting Your Own Online Business

Handling returns and refunds is an essential aspect of running a successful dropshipping business. As a dropshipper, you are responsible for ensuring that your customers are satisfied with their purchases, and that includes providing a smooth and hassle-free returns process. In this subchapter, we will discuss the best practices for handling returns and refunds to maintain customer satisfaction and protect your online reputation.

When it comes to handling returns, transparency is key. Make sure to clearly outline your return policy on your website so that customers know what to expect if they are not satisfied with their purchase. It is important to have a clear and easy-to-understand return policy that includes information on how to initiate a return, any restocking fees, and the timeframe for returns. By setting clear expectations upfront, you can avoid misunderstandings and customer dissatisfaction down the line.

Dropshipping 101: A Beginner's Guide to Starting Your Own Online Business

In the event that a customer requests a return, it is important to respond promptly and professionally. Make sure to provide clear instructions on how to return the item and any necessary documentation. It is also important to communicate with the customer throughout the returns process to keep them informed and address any concerns they may have. By providing excellent customer service during the returns process, you can turn a potentially negative experience into a positive one and retain customer loyalty.

Refunds are another aspect of handling returns that requires careful attention. When issuing a refund, make sure to do so promptly and accurately. It is important to process refunds in a timely manner to show customers that their satisfaction is a top priority. Additionally, make sure to communicate with the customer throughout the refund process to keep them informed of the status of their refund. By being transparent and responsive, you can build trust with your customers and encourage repeat business.

In conclusion, handling returns and refunds is an integral part of running a successful dropshipping business. By setting clear expectations, responding promptly and professionally, and communicating effectively with customers, you can ensure a positive experience for your customers and protect your online reputation. Remember, happy customers are more likely to become repeat customers and recommend your business to others, so make customer satisfaction a top priority in your dropshipping business.

Chapter 7: Dropshipping Marketing Tactics

Creating Compelling Product Descriptions

Creating compelling product descriptions is a crucial aspect of running a successful dropshipping business. Your product descriptions serve as the virtual sales pitch for your products, enticing potential customers to make a purchase. In this subchapter, we will explore the key elements of crafting product descriptions that capture the attention of your target audience and ultimately drive sales.

Dropshipping 101: A Beginner's Guide to Starting Your Own Online Business

When creating product descriptions, it is essential to highlight the unique features and benefits of each item. Clearly communicate what sets your products apart from others on the market and why customers should choose to buy from you. Use descriptive language that paints a vivid picture of the product, making it easy for customers to imagine themselves using it.

Dropshipping 101: A Beginner's Guide to Starting Your Own Online Business

In addition to highlighting the features of your products, it is also important to address any potential concerns or questions that customers may have. Anticipate common queries and provide detailed information to address them in your product descriptions. This will help build trust with your customers and increase the likelihood of making a sale.

Dropshipping 101: A Beginner's Guide to Starting Your Own Online Business

Another key aspect of creating compelling product descriptions is to incorporate keywords that are relevant to your niche. By optimizing your product descriptions with relevant keywords, you can improve your search engine rankings and attract more organic traffic to your online store. Be strategic in your use of keywords, ensuring that they flow naturally within the product description.

Lastly, don't forget to include a strong call-to-action in your product descriptions. Encourage customers to take the next step, whether it be making a purchase, signing up for a newsletter, or contacting customer support. A clear and compelling call-to-action can significantly increase your conversion rates and drive more sales for your dropshipping business. By following these tips and strategies for creating compelling product descriptions, you can enhance the shopping experience for your customers and boost the success of your dropshipping business.

Implementing Email Marketing Campaigns

Dropshipping 101: A Beginner's Guide to Starting Your Own Online Business

Implementing email marketing campaigns is a crucial aspect of running a successful dropshipping business. Email marketing allows you to reach out to potential customers, build relationships with existing ones, and ultimately drive sales. In this subchapter, we will discuss the key strategies and best practices for implementing effective email marketing campaigns in your dropshipping business.

Dropshipping 101: A Beginner's Guide to Starting Your Own Online Business

The first step in implementing email marketing campaigns is to build a list of subscribers. You can do this by offering incentives such as discounts, freebies, or exclusive content in exchange for email sign-ups. It's important to ensure that your subscribers have opted in to receive emails from you to comply with anti-spam laws and build trust with your audience.

Once you have a list of subscribers, you can start creating and sending out email campaigns. These campaigns can include promotional offers, product updates, newsletters, and more. It's important to segment your email list based on factors such as purchase history, preferences, and demographics to send targeted and relevant content to each subscriber.

Another key aspect of implementing email marketing campaigns is to track and analyze the performance of your emails. You can use email marketing software to monitor metrics such as open rates, click-through rates, conversion rates, and more. By analyzing these metrics, you can identify what is working well and what can be improved in your email campaigns.

In conclusion, implementing email marketing campaigns is an essential part of running a successful dropshipping business. By building a list of subscribers, creating targeted campaigns, and analyzing performance metrics, you can effectively reach out to potential customers, drive sales, and build lasting relationships with your audience. Email marketing is a powerful tool that can help you grow your dropshipping business and achieve long-term success.

Running Paid Advertising Campaigns

Running paid advertising campaigns is an essential aspect of successful dropshipping businesses. By investing in online ads, you can reach a larger audience and drive more traffic to your store. However, it's important to have a solid understanding of how paid advertising works and how to optimize your campaigns for maximum ROI.

Dropshipping 101: A Beginner's Guide to Starting Your Own Online Business

When it comes to running paid advertising campaigns, one of the first steps is to identify your target audience. This involves researching your niche market and understanding the demographics, interests, and behaviors of your potential customers. By knowing who your audience is, you can create more targeted ads that are likely to resonate with them and drive conversions.

Another important aspect of running paid advertising campaigns is choosing the right platform. There are various options available, such as Google Ads, Facebook Ads, and Instagram Ads. Each platform has its own strengths and weaknesses, so it's important to choose the one that best aligns with your business goals and target audience.

Dropshipping 101: A Beginner's Guide to Starting Your Own Online Business

Once you have selected a platform, it's crucial to set a budget for your advertising campaigns. Start with a small budget and test different ad creatives, targeting options, and messaging to see what works best for your business. As you gather data and insights, you can adjust your campaigns accordingly to optimize performance and maximize your ROI.

In conclusion, running paid advertising campaigns is a key component of successful dropshipping businesses. By identifying your target audience, choosing the right platform, setting a budget, and testing different strategies, you can drive more traffic to your store and increase your sales. With the right approach and ongoing optimization, paid advertising can be a powerful tool for growing your dropshipping business.

Influencer Partnerships and Affiliate Marketing

Influencer partnerships and affiliate marketing are two powerful tools that can help boost your dropshipping business to new heights. By collaborating with influencers in your niche, you can tap into their engaged audience and leverage their credibility to promote your products. This can lead to increased brand awareness, website traffic, and ultimately, sales. Affiliate marketing, on the other hand, involves partnering with individuals or companies who promote your products in exchange for a commission on each sale they generate. This can be a cost-effective way to drive sales, as you only pay for results.

Dropshipping 101: A Beginner's Guide to Starting Your Own Online Business

When choosing influencers to partner with, it's important to consider factors such as their reach, engagement rate, and alignment with your brand values. Look for influencers who have a genuine connection with their audience and whose followers are likely to be interested in your products. It's also important to establish clear expectations and guidelines for the partnership, including how the influencer will promote your products and how you will track the results.

Dropshipping 101: A Beginner's Guide to Starting Your Own Online Business

Affiliate marketing can be a great way to scale your dropshipping business without taking on additional marketing costs. By partnering with affiliates who have a strong online presence and a track record of driving sales, you can expand your reach and increase your sales revenue. It's important to provide affiliates with the tools and resources they need to effectively promote your products, such as banners, text links, and product images. You should also track the performance of your affiliate marketing efforts to identify top-performing affiliates and optimize your strategies.

Influencer partnerships and affiliate marketing can be powerful tools for driving sales and growing your dropshipping business. By strategically collaborating with influencers and affiliates who align with your brand values and target audience, you can tap into new markets and increase your revenue. It's important to establish clear expectations and guidelines for these partnerships, and to track their performance to ensure you're getting a good return on your investment. By leveraging the reach and credibility of influencers and affiliates, you can take your dropshipping business to the next level and achieve sustainable growth.

Chapter 8: Dropshipping Profit Margins and Pricing Strategies

Calculating Profit Margins

Calculating profit margins is a crucial aspect of running a successful dropshipping business. Understanding how to accurately determine your profit margins will help you make informed decisions about pricing, marketing strategies, and overall profitability. In this subchapter, we will break down the process of calculating profit margins and provide you with the tools you need to maximize your earnings.

Dropshipping 101: A Beginner's Guide to Starting Your Own Online Business

To calculate your profit margin, you first need to determine your total revenue and total costs. Total revenue is the sum of all the money you have made from sales, while total costs include expenses such as product costs, shipping fees, and marketing expenses. Once you have these figures, you can subtract your total costs from your total revenue to calculate your gross profit.

Once you have calculated your gross profit, you can then determine your profit margin by dividing your gross profit by your total revenue and multiplying the result by 100 to get a percentage. This percentage represents the proportion of your total revenue that is profit. It is important to regularly monitor and track your profit margins to ensure that your business remains profitable and sustainable.

There are several strategies you can use to improve your profit margins, such as negotiating better terms with suppliers, optimizing your pricing strategy, and reducing overhead costs. By continuously evaluating and adjusting your profit margins, you can increase your bottom line and grow your dropshipping business effectively.

In conclusion, calculating profit margins is an essential skill for any dropshipper looking to succeed in the competitive e-commerce market. By understanding how to accurately determine your profit margins and implementing strategies to improve them, you can make informed decisions that will drive your business's success. Remember to regularly assess your profit margins and make adjustments as needed to ensure long-term profitability and growth.

Setting Competitive Prices

Dropshipping 101: A Beginner's Guide to Starting Your Own Online Business

Setting competitive prices is a crucial aspect of running a successful dropshipping business. When it comes to pricing your products, it's important to strike a balance between profitability and competitiveness. Your pricing strategy can have a significant impact on your sales and overall success in the market. In this section, we will discuss some key considerations for setting competitive prices in your dropshipping business.

One of the first steps in setting competitive prices is to research your competitors. Take the time to analyze the pricing strategies of other businesses in your niche. This will give you a better understanding of the market and help you determine a pricing strategy that will set you apart from the competition. By knowing what your competitors are charging for similar products, you can adjust your prices accordingly to remain competitive.

Another important factor to consider when setting prices is your profit margins. While it's important to offer competitive prices to attract customers, you also need to ensure that you are making a profit on each sale. Calculate your costs, including product costs, shipping fees, and any other expenses, and determine the minimum price you need to charge to maintain a healthy profit margin.

It's also important to consider the perceived value of your products when setting prices. Customers are willing to pay more for products that they perceive to be of higher quality or value. By highlighting the unique features or benefits of your products, you can justify pricing them higher than your competitors. This can help you differentiate your business and attract customers who are willing to pay a premium for your products.

Dropshipping 101: A Beginner's Guide to Starting Your Own Online Business

In addition to researching competitors, calculating profit margins, and considering perceived value, you should also regularly monitor and adjust your prices based on market trends and customer feedback. Pricing is not a one-time decision, but an ongoing process that requires constant evaluation and adjustment. By staying informed about market trends and customer preferences, you can ensure that your prices remain competitive and profitable in the long run.

In conclusion, setting competitive prices is a critical aspect of running a successful dropshipping business. By researching competitors, calculating profit margins, considering perceived value, and monitoring market trends, you can develop a pricing strategy that attracts customers and drives sales. Remember that pricing is not set in stone and should be regularly evaluated and adjusted to remain competitive in the ever-changing dropshipping market.

Utilizing Dynamic Pricing Strategies

Dropshipping 101: A Beginner's Guide to Starting Your Own Online Business

Utilizing dynamic pricing strategies is a key component of running a successful dropshipping business. Dynamic pricing allows you to adjust the prices of your products in real-time based on factors such as demand, competition, and seasonality. By implementing dynamic pricing strategies, you can maximize your profits and stay ahead of the competition.

Dropshipping 101: A Beginner's Guide to Starting Your Own Online Business

One effective dynamic pricing strategy is to use price tracking tools to monitor the prices of your competitors. By keeping an eye on what your competitors are charging for similar products, you can adjust your prices accordingly to remain competitive. This can help you attract more customers and increase your sales.

Another dynamic pricing strategy is to implement a tiered pricing structure based on customer behavior. For example, you can offer discounts to customers who purchase multiple items or who have been loyal customers for a certain period of time. This can help increase customer retention and encourage repeat business.

Dropshipping 101: A Beginner's Guide to Starting Your Own Online Business

In addition to monitoring your competitors and implementing a tiered pricing structure, you can also use dynamic pricing to capitalize on seasonal trends and demand fluctuations. By adjusting your prices during peak seasons or times of high demand, you can maximize your profits and take advantage of market opportunities.

Overall, dynamic pricing strategies are essential for success in the competitive world of dropshipping. By staying flexible and adapting your pricing strategies based on market conditions, competition, and customer behavior, you can increase your profits and grow your business. Make sure to continually evaluate and refine your dynamic pricing strategies to stay ahead of the competition and achieve long-term success in the dropshipping industry.

Monitoring and Adjusting Prices

Monitoring and adjusting prices is a crucial aspect of running a successful dropshipping business. It involves keeping a close eye on market trends, competitor pricing, and customer demand to ensure that your prices remain competitive and profitable. By regularly monitoring and adjusting your prices, you can maximize your profits and stay ahead of the competition.

Dropshipping 101: A Beginner's Guide to Starting Your Own Online Business

One of the key benefits of monitoring and adjusting prices is that it allows you to stay competitive in the market. By keeping a close eye on what your competitors are charging for similar products, you can adjust your prices accordingly to attract customers and drive sales. This can help you stay ahead of the competition and position your business as a leader in your niche.

Dropshipping 101: A Beginner's Guide to Starting Your Own Online Business

Additionally, monitoring and adjusting prices can help you maximize your profits. By regularly analyzing your pricing strategy and making adjustments as needed, you can ensure that you are charging the right amount for your products to cover your costs and generate a healthy profit margin. This can help you grow your business and increase your bottom line over time.

Another benefit of monitoring and adjusting prices is that it allows you to respond quickly to changes in customer demand. By keeping a close eye on which products are selling well and which are not, you can adjust your prices to capitalize on trends and meet customer needs. This can help you stay relevant in the market and attract new customers to your business.

In conclusion, monitoring and adjusting prices is an essential part of running a successful dropshipping business. By staying on top of market trends, competitor pricing, and customer demand, you can ensure that your prices remain competitive and profitable. By regularly analyzing your pricing strategy and making adjustments as needed, you can maximize your profits, stay ahead of the competition, and respond quickly to changes in customer demand.

Chapter 9: Dropshipping Customer Service and Satisfaction

Providing Excellent Customer Support

In the world of dropshipping, providing excellent customer support is essential for the success of your online business. Whether you are a beginner just starting out or an experienced dropshipper looking to take your business to the next level, focusing on customer service can set you apart from the competition.

Dropshipping 101: A Beginner's Guide to Starting Your Own Online Business

One of the key aspects of providing excellent customer support is being responsive to inquiries and concerns. Make sure to promptly respond to customer emails, messages, and phone calls to show that you value their business. By being attentive and addressing any issues in a timely manner, you can build trust and loyalty with your customers.

Dropshipping 101: A Beginner's Guide to Starting Your Own Online Business

Another important aspect of customer support is ensuring that your customers are satisfied with their purchases. This can involve offering refunds or exchanges for faulty products, providing tracking information for orders, and offering assistance with returns or exchanges. By going above and beyond to meet your customers' needs, you can create a positive shopping experience that encourages repeat business.

Dropshipping 101: A Beginner's Guide to Starting Your Own Online Business

It is also important to communicate clearly with your customers throughout the buying process. Provide detailed product descriptions, shipping information, and return policies on your website to help customers make informed decisions. Additionally, keep customers updated on the status of their orders and provide tracking information so they know when to expect their purchases.

By focusing on providing excellent customer support, you can differentiate your dropshipping business from competitors and build a loyal customer base. Remember that happy customers are more likely to recommend your business to others and return for future purchases. By prioritizing customer satisfaction, you can create a positive shopping experience that sets you up for long-term success in the world of dropshipping.

Handling Customer Inquiries and Complaints

Dropshipping 101: A Beginner's Guide to Starting Your Own Online Business

Handling customer inquiries and complaints is a crucial aspect of running a successful dropshipping business. As a dropshipper, you will inevitably encounter situations where customers have questions, concerns, or issues with their orders. It is important to have a well-defined process in place to address these inquiries and complaints effectively.

Dropshipping 101: A Beginner's Guide to Starting Your Own Online Business

First and foremost, it is essential to respond to customer inquiries promptly. Customers expect quick and timely responses, so make sure to check your email and messages regularly. If a customer reaches out with a question or concern, acknowledge their inquiry and provide them with a clear and helpful response. This will show your customers that you value their business and are committed to providing excellent customer service.

Dropshipping 101: A Beginner's Guide to Starting Your Own Online Business

In the event that a customer has a complaint about their order, it is important to handle the situation with empathy and professionalism. Listen to the customer's concerns and try to understand their perspective. Apologize for any inconvenience they may have experienced and offer a resolution to their problem. Whether it be a refund, replacement, or another form of compensation, make sure to address the issue promptly and effectively to ensure customer satisfaction.

In addition to addressing individual customer inquiries and complaints, it is also important to look for trends or common issues that may arise. Keep track of the types of inquiries and complaints you receive and work to address any recurring issues. By identifying and resolving these issues proactively, you can improve the overall customer experience and reduce the likelihood of future complaints.

Dropshipping 101: A Beginner's Guide to Starting Your Own Online Business

Furthermore, consider implementing customer feedback surveys or follow-up emails to gather insights on how you can improve your products and services. By actively seeking feedback from customers, you can demonstrate your commitment to continuous improvement and customer satisfaction. Use this feedback to make necessary adjustments to your dropshipping business and enhance the overall customer experience.

In conclusion, handling customer inquiries and complaints is an essential part of running a successful dropshipping business. By responding promptly, addressing complaints with empathy and professionalism, identifying trends, and seeking customer feedback, you can improve the overall customer experience and build a loyal customer base. Remember that excellent customer service is key to long-term success in the dropshipping industry.

Building Trust and Loyalty

Dropshipping 101: A Beginner's Guide to Starting Your Own Online Business

Building trust and loyalty are crucial aspects of running a successful dropshipping business. In the competitive online marketplace, gaining the trust of your customers is essential for building a loyal customer base that will keep coming back for more. Trust can be built through various strategies, such as offering high-quality products, providing excellent customer service, and being transparent about your business practices.

Dropshipping 101: A Beginner's Guide to Starting Your Own Online Business

One important way to build trust with your customers is by ensuring the quality of the products you offer. It is essential to work with reliable suppliers who can provide high-quality products that meet the expectations of your customers. By offering products that are well-made and durable, you can build trust with your customers and establish a positive reputation for your business.

Another key aspect of building trust and loyalty is providing excellent customer service. Responding promptly to customer inquiries, resolving any issues or complaints quickly, and going above and beyond to make sure your customers are satisfied can help build a strong relationship with your customers. By showing that you care about their experience and are willing to go the extra mile to ensure their satisfaction, you can build trust and loyalty with your customers.

Transparency is also crucial in building trust with your customers. Being honest about your business practices, including your shipping times, return policies, and pricing strategies, can help build trust with your customers. By being upfront and transparent about how your business operates, you can build credibility and establish trust with your customers.

Overall, building trust and loyalty with your customers is essential for the success of your dropshipping business. By offering high-quality products, providing excellent customer service, and being transparent about your business practices, you can build a loyal customer base that will keep coming back for more. Building trust and loyalty takes time and effort, but the rewards of having a strong and loyal customer base are well worth it in the long run.

Encouraging Positive Reviews and Feedback

Dropshipping 101: A Beginner's Guide to Starting Your Own Online Business

Encouraging positive reviews and feedback is essential for the success of your dropshipping business. Positive reviews and feedback not only help build trust with potential customers, but they also improve your brand's reputation and credibility in the marketplace. In this subchapter, we will discuss strategies and tips for encouraging positive reviews and feedback from your customers.

One of the best ways to encourage positive reviews and feedback is to provide excellent customer service. Respond promptly to customer inquiries and resolve any issues or concerns they may have in a timely and professional manner. By providing exceptional customer service, you are more likely to receive positive reviews and feedback from satisfied customers.

Another effective way to encourage positive reviews and feedback is to offer incentives to customers who leave reviews. Consider offering discounts, freebies, or other rewards to customers who take the time to leave a review of their purchase. This not only incentivizes customers to leave feedback but also shows that you value their opinions and feedback.

Additionally, make it easy for customers to leave reviews by providing multiple channels for feedback, such as email, social media, and your website. Encourage customers to leave reviews by sending follow-up emails after their purchase, asking for their feedback and inviting them to share their experience with others.

Dropshipping 101: A Beginner's Guide to Starting Your Own Online Business

Lastly, showcase positive reviews and feedback on your website and social media channels. Displaying testimonials and reviews from satisfied customers can help build credibility and trust with potential customers. Consider creating a dedicated page on your website for customer reviews or sharing positive feedback on social media to showcase the positive experiences of your customers. By following these strategies and tips, you can encourage positive reviews and feedback for your dropshipping business, ultimately helping you build a strong reputation and attract more customers.

Chapter 10: Dropshipping Automation Tools and Software

Order Management Systems

Order management systems are crucial for the success of any dropshipping business. These systems help streamline the process of receiving, processing, and fulfilling orders from customers. By implementing an order management system, you can efficiently track orders, manage inventory, and ensure timely delivery of products to customers.

One of the key benefits of using an order management system is that it helps you avoid overselling products. With real-time inventory tracking, you can easily see how many units of each product are available for sale. This prevents the frustration of having to cancel orders due to lack of stock, and helps maintain a positive customer experience.

Order management systems also enable you to automate the order processing and fulfillment process. By setting up rules and workflows within the system, you can automatically route orders to the appropriate suppliers, generate shipping labels, and send tracking information to customers. This automation saves time and reduces the risk of human error in the order fulfillment process.

Dropshipping 101: A Beginner's Guide to Starting Your Own Online Business

In addition to order processing and fulfillment, order management systems provide valuable insights into your sales performance. By tracking key metrics such as order volume, average order value, and order fulfillment time, you can identify trends and make data-driven decisions to optimize your dropshipping business.

Overall, implementing an order management system is essential for scaling your dropshipping business and providing a seamless shopping experience for your customers. Whether you are just starting out or looking to streamline your operations, investing in a reliable order management system is a smart decision for any dropshipper.

Inventory Management Software

Inventory management software is an essential tool for any dropshipping business looking to streamline operations and increase efficiency. This software allows you to keep track of your inventory in real-time, helping you avoid stockouts and overstock situations that can harm your bottom line. By using inventory management software, you can easily track product levels, set up automatic reordering, and generate reports to help you make data-driven decisions about your inventory.

Dropshipping 101: A Beginner's Guide to Starting Your Own Online Business

One of the key benefits of inventory management software is its ability to integrate with your dropshipping platform, such as Shopify or Amazon. This integration allows for seamless communication between your sales channels and your inventory, ensuring that you always have the right products in stock to fulfill customer orders. By automating these processes, you can save time and reduce the risk of human error, ultimately improving customer satisfaction and increasing sales.

Additionally, inventory management software can help you optimize your supply chain by providing insights into which products are selling well and which ones are not. By analyzing this data, you can make informed decisions about which products to focus on and which ones to discontinue. This can help you maximize your profits and minimize waste, ultimately leading to a more successful dropshipping business.

Dropshipping 101: A Beginner's Guide to Starting Your Own Online Business

Another advantage of inventory management software is its ability to track product performance and customer demand. By analyzing sales trends and customer behavior, you can identify which products are popular and which ones are not resonating with your target audience. This information can help you make informed decisions about which products to promote and which ones to phase out, ultimately increasing your sales and profits.

In conclusion, inventory management software is a powerful tool that can help you optimize your dropshipping business and achieve greater success. By using this software to track inventory levels, integrate with your sales channels, optimize your supply chain, and analyze sales trends, you can make data-driven decisions that will drive your business forward. Whether you are a beginner or an experienced dropshipper, investing in inventory management software is a smart choice that can help you take your business to the next level.

Marketing Automation Tools

Marketing automation tools are essential for any dropshipping business looking to streamline their processes and increase efficiency. These tools help automate repetitive tasks such as email marketing, social media scheduling, and customer relationship management. By using marketing automation tools, dropshippers can save time and focus on more strategic aspects of their business.

Dropshipping 101: A Beginner's Guide to Starting Your Own Online Business

One popular marketing automation tool for dropshippers is Mailchimp. Mailchimp allows users to create automated email campaigns, segment their audience, and track the performance of their campaigns. This tool is especially useful for nurturing leads and converting them into customers. With Mailchimp, dropshippers can create personalized and targeted email campaigns that drive sales and increase customer engagement.

Another valuable marketing automation tool for dropshippers is Hootsuite. Hootsuite is a social media management platform that allows users to schedule posts, monitor social media activity, and analyze performance metrics. By using Hootsuite, dropshippers can save time by scheduling posts in advance and engaging with their audience in real-time. This tool is especially useful for maintaining a consistent social media presence and building brand awareness.

In addition to Mailchimp and Hootsuite, dropshippers can also benefit from using tools such as HubSpot, Klaviyo, and ActiveCampaign. These tools offer a wide range of features including lead generation, customer segmentation, and automated workflows. By leveraging these marketing automation tools, dropshippers can attract more customers, improve brand loyalty, and increase sales.

Overall, marketing automation tools are essential for dropshippers looking to scale their business and achieve long-term success. By automating repetitive tasks and streamlining processes, dropshippers can focus on growing their business and delivering a seamless customer experience. Whether you are a beginner or an experienced dropshipper, investing in marketing automation tools is key to staying competitive in the ever-evolving e-commerce landscape.

Customer Relationship Management (CRM) Software

Dropshipping 101: A Beginner's Guide to Starting Your Own Online Business

Customer Relationship Management (CRM) software plays a crucial role in the success of any dropshipping business. This type of software is designed to help businesses manage and analyze their interactions with customers, ultimately helping to build stronger relationships and increase sales. CRM software can track customer interactions, store important customer data, and provide valuable insights into customer behavior and preferences.

Dropshipping 101: A Beginner's Guide to Starting Your Own Online Business

One of the key benefits of using CRM software in a dropshipping business is the ability to personalize the customer experience. By tracking customer interactions and preferences, businesses can tailor their marketing efforts and product recommendations to individual customers. This personalization can help increase customer loyalty and retention, ultimately leading to higher sales and profits.

CRM software also enables businesses to better understand their customers and their needs. By analyzing customer data, businesses can identify trends and patterns that can help them make more informed decisions about their products and marketing strategies. This data-driven approach can lead to more targeted marketing campaigns and more successful product offerings.

In addition to helping businesses manage their customer relationships, CRM software can also streamline internal processes and improve overall efficiency. By centralizing customer data and communication channels, businesses can reduce manual tasks and eliminate the need for multiple, disconnected systems. This can lead to faster response times, improved customer service, and a more cohesive overall business operation.

Overall, CRM software is an essential tool for any dropshipping business looking to build strong customer relationships, increase sales, and improve efficiency. By investing in a quality CRM system, businesses can gain valuable insights into their customers, personalize their marketing efforts, and ultimately drive long-term success in the competitive world of online retail.

Chapter 11: Dropshipping Success Stories and Case Studies

Case Study: How I Started My Own Dropshipping Business

Dropshipping 101: A Beginner's Guide to Starting Your Own Online Business

In this case study, I will share my personal journey of how I started my own dropshipping business. It all began with my interest in entrepreneurship and the desire to create a flexible and profitable online business. After researching various online business models, I came across dropshipping and was intrigued by its low start-up costs and potential for high profits.

Dropshipping 101: A Beginner's Guide to Starting Your Own Online Business

I started by conducting thorough market research to identify a profitable niche for my dropshipping business. I analyzed trends, competition, and customer demand to narrow down my choices. Once I found a niche that showed promise, I set up my online store using a platform like Shopify or Amazon, which made it easy to list products and manage orders.

Next, I focused on sourcing high-quality products from reliable suppliers to ensure customer satisfaction and build a positive reputation for my brand. I leveraged dropshipping automation tools and software to streamline order processing and inventory management, allowing me to focus on growing my business and expanding my product line.

Dropshipping 101: A Beginner's Guide to Starting Your Own Online Business

To attract customers and drive sales, I implemented various marketing tactics such as social media advertising, email campaigns, and search engine optimization. I also optimized my pricing strategies to maintain competitive prices while maximizing profit margins. Providing excellent customer service and ensuring customer satisfaction were top priorities for me, as positive reviews and word-of-mouth referrals were essential for building trust and loyalty among my customers.

Through dedication, hard work, and strategic decision-making, my dropshipping business began to thrive. I learned valuable lessons along the way and continuously adapted my strategies to stay ahead in the competitive online marketplace. This case study serves as a testament to the potential of dropshipping as a lucrative and rewarding business model for aspiring entrepreneurs in the digital age.

Success Story: Top Dropshipping Entrepreneurs to Follow

Dropshipping 101: A Beginner's Guide to Starting Your Own Online Business

Success stories can be incredibly inspiring for those looking to start their own dropshipping business. In this subchapter, we will highlight some of the top dropshipping entrepreneurs that you should follow for guidance and motivation. These entrepreneurs have proven themselves in the industry and have valuable insights to share with aspiring business owners.

Dropshipping 101: A Beginner's Guide to Starting Your Own Online Business

One top dropshipping entrepreneur to follow is Sarah, who started her online business with just a few products and a limited budget. Through strategic marketing tactics and a keen eye for trending products, Sarah was able to grow her business exponentially within a short period of time. By staying on top of industry trends and constantly adapting her strategies, Sarah was able to achieve great success in the dropshipping world.

Dropshipping 101: A Beginner's Guide to Starting Your Own Online Business

Another entrepreneur to watch is Mike, who has mastered the art of dropshipping on specific platforms such as Shopify and Amazon. Mike's success can be attributed to his deep understanding of these platforms and his ability to optimize his listings for maximum visibility and sales. By leveraging the tools and resources available on these platforms, Mike was able to streamline his operations and increase his profit margins significantly.

Additionally, Emily is a dropshipping entrepreneur who has excelled in niche selection and product sourcing. By focusing on a specific niche and carefully curating her product selection, Emily was able to attract a loyal customer base and establish herself as a trusted authority in her industry. Through strategic partnerships with suppliers and diligent research, Emily was able to consistently offer high-quality products to her customers.

These success stories serve as a reminder that with dedication, hard work, and a strategic approach, anyone can achieve success in the world of dropshipping. By following the example set by these top entrepreneurs and learning from their experiences, you too can build a successful dropshipping business. Stay tuned for more insights and tips from these top dropshipping entrepreneurs as we delve deeper into their strategies and success stories in the following chapters.

Lessons Learned from Successful Dropshipping Businesses

Dropshipping 101: A Beginner's Guide to Starting Your Own Online Business

In the world of dropshipping, there are countless success stories that can serve as valuable lessons for aspiring entrepreneurs. By studying the strategies and tactics employed by these successful businesses, we can gain insight into what it takes to thrive in the competitive world of online retail. From niche selection to marketing tactics, there are many key takeaways that can help guide new dropshippers on their path to success.

Dropshipping 101: A Beginner's Guide to Starting Your Own Online Business

One important lesson learned from successful dropshipping businesses is the importance of choosing the right niche. By selecting a niche with high demand and low competition, businesses can increase their chances of success. Additionally, focusing on a niche that aligns with your interests and expertise can help you stand out in a crowded market.

Dropshipping 101: A Beginner's Guide to Starting Your Own Online Business

Another key lesson is the importance of effective marketing tactics. Successful dropshipping businesses understand the value of building a strong online presence through social media, email marketing, and other digital channels. By creating engaging content and targeting the right audience, businesses can drive traffic to their online store and increase sales.

Successful dropshippers also prioritize customer service and satisfaction. By providing excellent customer support and addressing any issues promptly, businesses can build trust and loyalty with their customers. This can lead to repeat business and positive word-of-mouth referrals, which are essential for long-term success.

Overall, the lessons learned from successful dropshipping businesses highlight the importance of careful planning, strategic decision-making, and a strong focus on customer satisfaction. By incorporating these principles into your own dropshipping business, you can increase your chances of achieving sustainable growth and success in the competitive world of online retail.

Tips for Achieving Dropshipping Success

Achieving success in dropshipping requires a combination of strategy, hard work, and dedication. Here are some tips to help you on your journey to becoming a successful dropshipper.

First and foremost, it's important to choose the right niche for your dropshipping business. Research different niches to find one that is not only profitable but also aligns with your interests and expertise. This will make it easier for you to market and sell products within that niche.

Once you have chosen a niche, it's crucial to focus on product sourcing. Look for reliable suppliers who can provide high-quality products at competitive prices. Building strong relationships with your suppliers will help ensure smooth operations and timely deliveries to your customers.

Dropshipping 101: A Beginner's Guide to Starting Your Own Online Business

Marketing is key to the success of any dropshipping business. Utilize various marketing tactics such as social media advertising, email marketing, and search engine optimization to drive traffic to your online store. Engage with your target audience and build relationships with potential customers to increase sales and grow your business.

Another important aspect of dropshipping success is providing excellent customer service. Respond to customer inquiries promptly, address any issues or concerns, and strive to exceed customer expectations. Happy customers are more likely to become repeat customers and recommend your business to others.

Lastly, consider using automation tools and software to streamline your dropshipping operations. Automating tasks such as order processing, inventory management, and customer communication can save you time and help you focus on growing your business. By following these tips and staying committed to your goals, you can achieve dropshipping success and build a profitable online business.

This book is designed to provide a comprehensive guide to dropshipping for beginners, covering everything from the basics of how dropshipping works to advanced strategies for success.

Whether you are just starting out in the world of online business or looking to take your dropshipping business to the next level, this book has something for every person interested in dropshipping.

Dropshipping 101: A Beginner's Guide to Starting Your Own Online Business

In the first section of the book, we will delve into the fundamentals of dropshipping, exploring what it is and how it works. We will discuss the benefits of dropshipping, such as low startup costs and the ability to run your business from anywhere in the world. Additionally, we will cover common misconceptions about dropshipping and how to avoid pitfalls that many beginners encounter.

Dropshipping 101: A Beginner's Guide to Starting Your Own Online Business

For those who are new to dropshipping, we have a dedicated chapter that will walk you through the process step by step. From setting up your online store to finding reliable suppliers and marketing your products effectively, this section will provide you with all the information you need to get started on the right foot. We will also discuss how to choose the right niche for your dropshipping business and how to source high-quality products that will attract customers.

Dropshipping 101: A Beginner's Guide to Starting Your Own Online Business

Once you have mastered the basics, we will move on to advanced dropshipping strategies that can help you scale your business and increase your profits. We will explore techniques for optimizing your product listings, leveraging automation tools and software, and building a strong brand that resonates with your target audience. Additionally, we will share success stories and case studies from experienced dropshippers who have achieved remarkable results in the industry.

Dropshipping 101: A Beginner's Guide to Starting Your Own Online Business

Lastly, we will cover specific platforms where you can set up your dropshipping business, such as Shopify and Amazon. We will discuss the unique features of each platform, as well as tips and tricks for maximizing your success on these popular e-commerce sites. Whether you are a beginner looking to launch your first online store or an experienced dropshipper seeking new opportunities, this book will provide you with the knowledge and tools you need to thrive in the world of dropshipping.

About me.

Meet Stephanie, an incredible individual who has dealt with generalized epilepsy since birth. She is happily married to her best friend of over 20 years and is a devoted parent to three exceptional children, two of whom have special needs. With more than 15 years of experience working for a church, she has served as a youth pastor and worked with young adults. Stephanie firmly believes in the power of love and hard work in relationships. Reflecting on her journey, she wishes there had been a helpful book like this when she needed guidance for moms who wanted to make money without falling for scams. She is confident that this book will empower you to be brave and venture into new opportunities.ortor.

www.ingramcontent.com/pod-product-compliance
Lightning Source LLC
LaVergne TN
LVHW081523050326
832903LV00025B/1611